A NATURAL HISTORY OF BUMS

THE STORY OF EVOLUTION, FROM YOUR BUM TO BEYOND

Written by Crab Museum Co-Director,
Bertie Terrilliams

Illustrated by Inga Ziemele

WIDE EYED EDITIONS

Armored bum

Bum that explodes acid

Bum full of eggs

Mouth bum

For hundreds of millions of years, bums have given animals the strength to take over the world. Bums are a record of everything that has ever been. If we listen to them, they can tell us about the future, too. That's right—the humble bum is packed full of science! And farts, obviously. Are you sitting comfortably? Yes, you are—because of your bum!

WHAT'S THE POINT OF A BUM?

There are millions of different animals on Earth, and they each have amazing and unique bums. There are many kinds of bums that all have very different jobs. And these jobs are important—animals just wouldn't be able to do the things they do without their bums.

JOBS FOR BUMS

Moving around, like the young dragonflies that suck water up their bums and fart themselves forward

Breathing, like the river turtles that absorb oxygen through their bums while underwater

Protecting against predators, like the honey badgers that squirt smelly goop from their bums to warn off other animals

AND OTHER JOBS, LIKE . . .
- Eating through it
- Peeing out of it
- Laying eggs with it
- Looking good in jeans
- Sending messages

I use mine as a pencil sharpener!

BUT WHAT *IS* A BUM?

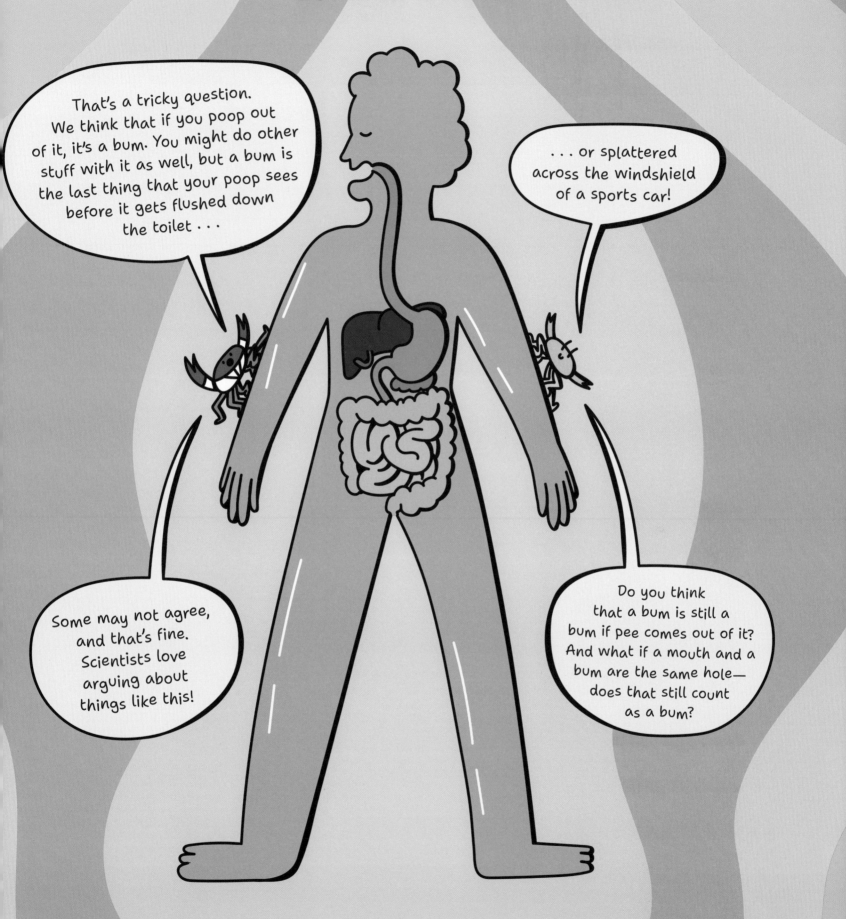

BUMS = LIFE

So, how did animals get all these amazing bums?

Things have changed a lot since life on Earth started. Animals have kept changing, too—this is called "evolution," and it can take a really long time. Like, millions and millions of years. And it means that animals are always working on exciting new bottoms!

You got your bum from your parents. They got their bums from *their* parents, and so on. But if you go back far enough, your ancestors had monkey bums. If you keep going back even further, bums start looking very different.

We can use bums to see how animals came to be the way they are today. We can learn about the animals that died out long ago, and the animals that slowly changed into other things.

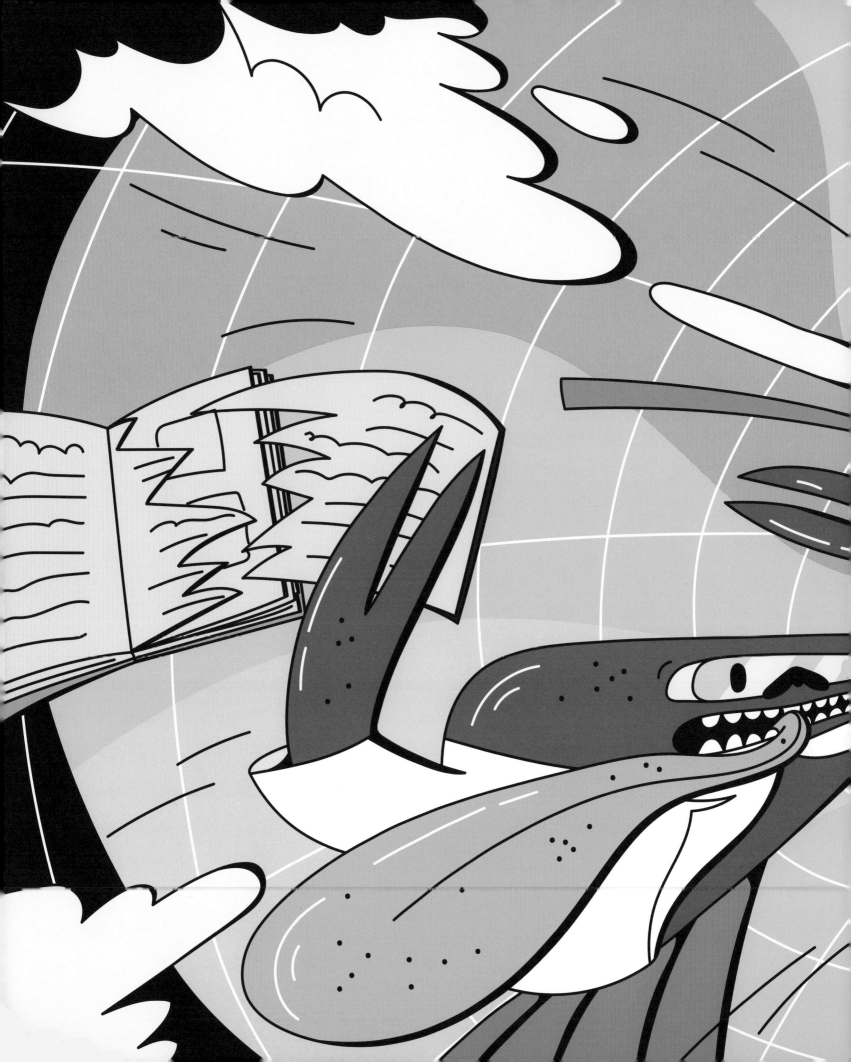

THE BEGINNING OF LIFE

In the beginning . . . there were no bums!

When life started on Earth, things were much simpler. There weren't any animals at all yet. There were just single-celled blobs, like bacteria floating in the sea.

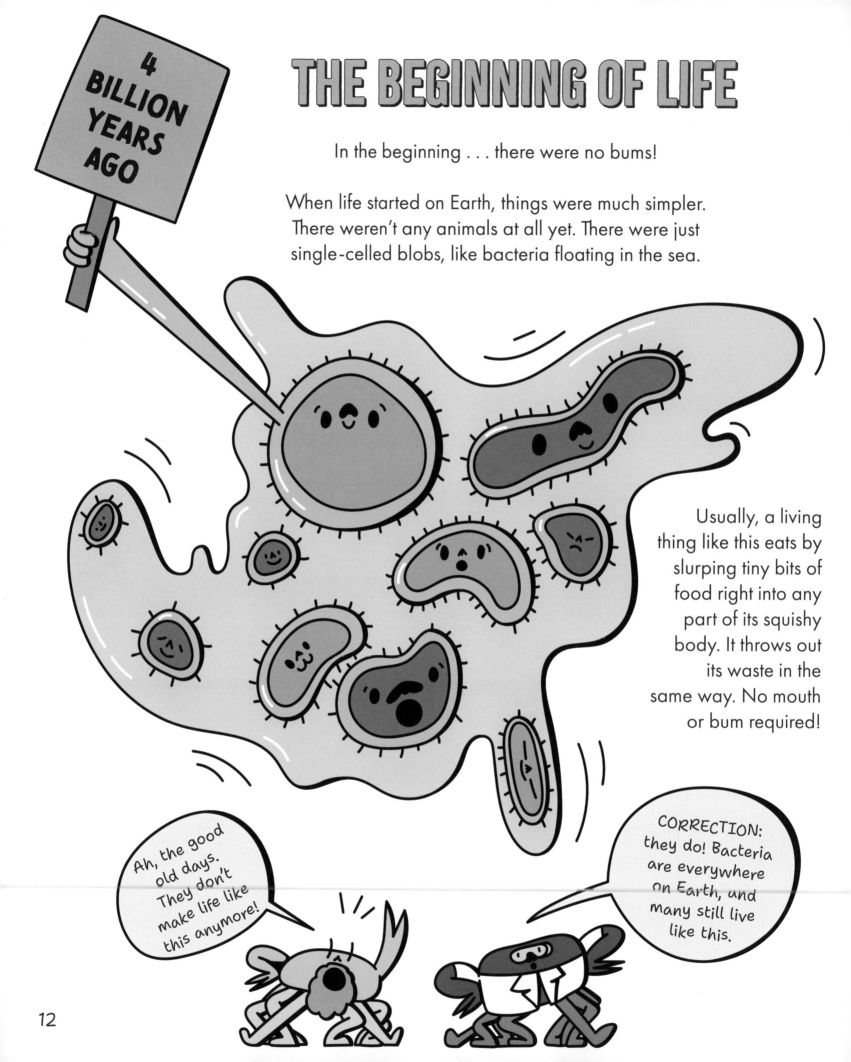

4 BILLION YEARS AGO

Usually, a living thing like this eats by slurping tiny bits of food right into any part of its squishy body. It throws out its waste in the same way. No mouth or bum required!

Ah, the good old days. They don't make life like this anymore!

CORRECTION: they do! Bacteria are everywhere on Earth, and many still live like this.

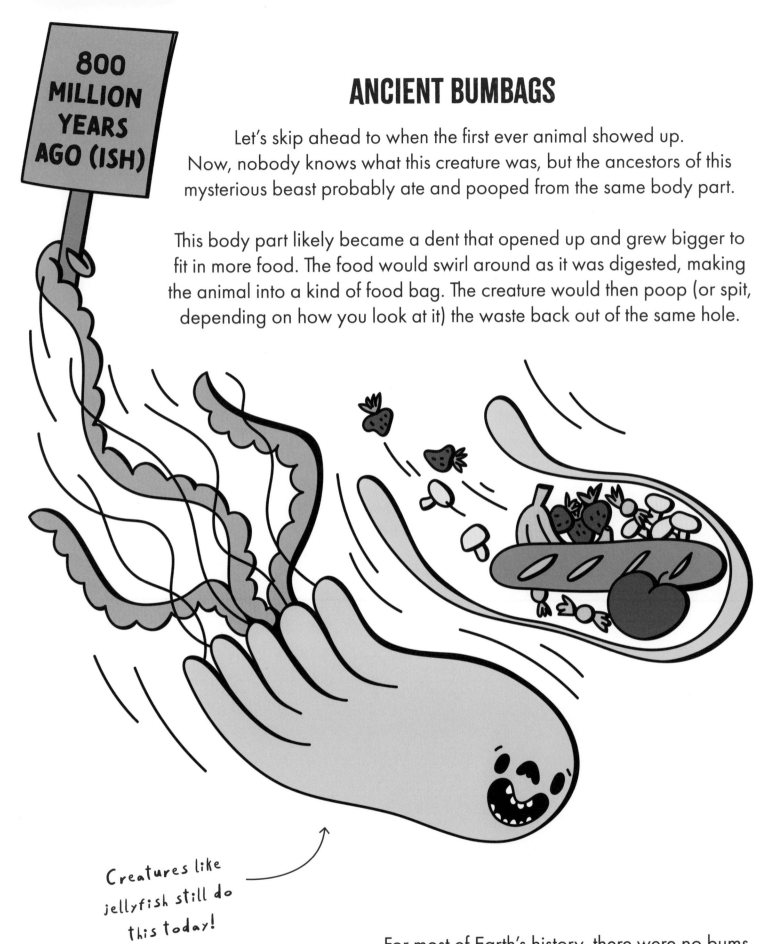

ANCIENT BUMBAGS

Let's skip ahead to when the first ever animal showed up.
Now, nobody knows what this creature was, but the ancestors of this
mysterious beast probably ate and pooped from the same body part.

This body part likely became a dent that opened up and grew bigger to
fit in more food. The food would swirl around as it was digested, making
the animal into a kind of food bag. The creature would then poop (or spit,
depending on how you look at it) the waste back out of the same hole.

800 MILLION YEARS AGO (ISH)

Creatures like
jellyfish still do
this today!

For most of Earth's history, there were no bums
at all. That's right—patooties are pretty
recent inventions.

BIRTH OF THE BOOTY

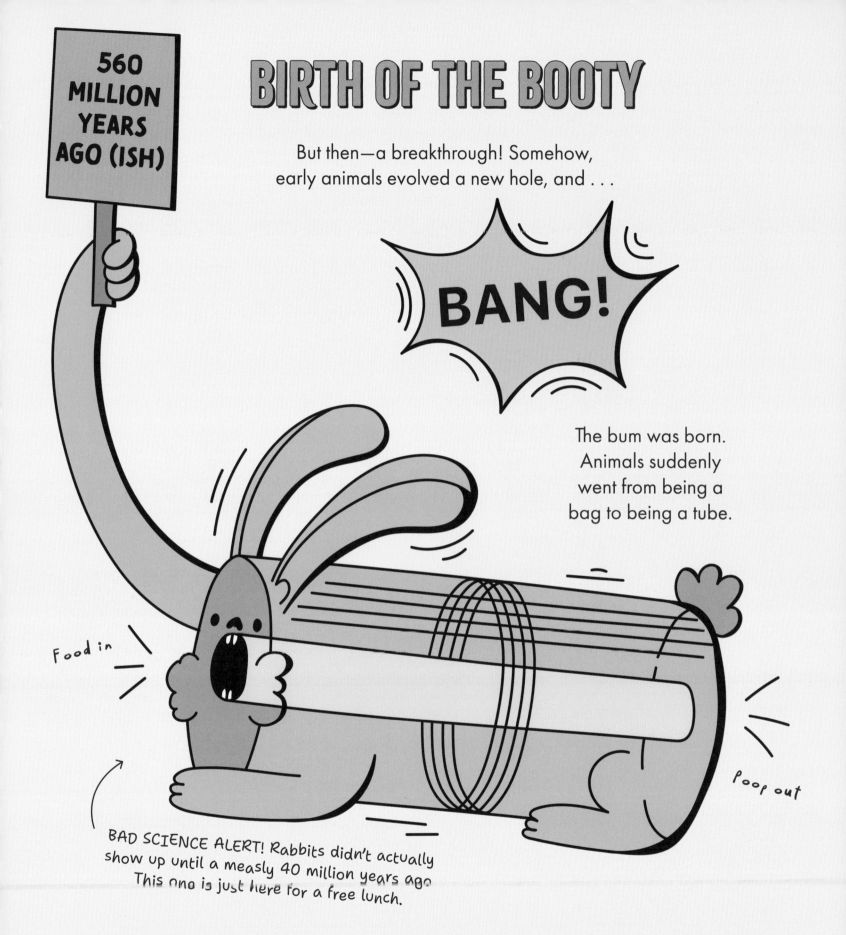

560 MILLION YEARS AGO (ISH)

But then—a breakthrough! Somehow, early animals evolved a new hole, and . . .

BANG!

The bum was born. Animals suddenly went from being a bag to being a tube.

Food in

Poop out

BAD SCIENCE ALERT! Rabbits didn't actually show up until a measly 40 million years ago. This one is just here for a free lunch.

We'll meet an early bum-owner pretty soon. First, let's find out why bums are all they're *cracked* up to be. Cracked . . . like, bum crack? Got that one? Alright, just making sure.

Having a bum means that you can eat and poop from different ends. You don't need to be empty before you can eat again. You can just keep eating and pooping at the same time. We are all food tubes, whether we're crab scientists or human readers!

Being a tube means that you can eat much more food, which means you have more energy to grow bigger.

NOT JUST A TUSH

When an animal is a tube, it has a front and a back and a left and a right. The fancy word for this is *bilateral*.

How does a bilateral animal find food to stuff into the front end of its tube? Well, by growing things to help it move around. All of our body parts are accessories that help the mouth end of the tube find more food.

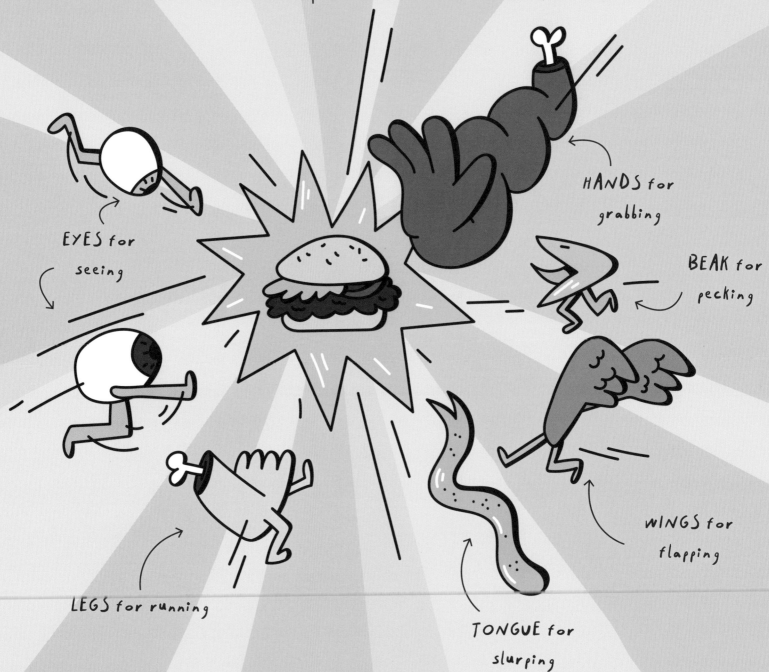

EYES for seeing

HANDS for grabbing

BEAK for pecking

WINGS for flapping

LEGS for running

TONGUE for slurping

BUMS GET BRAINY

Once an animal has accessories like eyes and hands, it needs to make sense of all the new things it can see and touch. That means it needs a brain! The more complicated an animal's body becomes, the more complicated its brain has to be to keep everything working.

For example, here are two food tubes each looking for their dinner.

Both use their brains, eyes, and sense of smell to find food. Both will run toward it with their legs, and will push others out of the way if they have to. Both will squeeze it out of their bum when they've finished. They're not so different!

BUM EVOLUTION

But wait—how do animals get all these new eyes and brains and stuff?

They evolve!

Every animal has features that make it different from every other animal on the planet. Its features can be useful, like a bum that helps a creature hide from predators. But they can also be not so useful, like a bright red bum that predators find extra delicious. The animal with the most useful features survives and has babies. Over time, an animal's descendants evolve to become better and better suited to where they live.

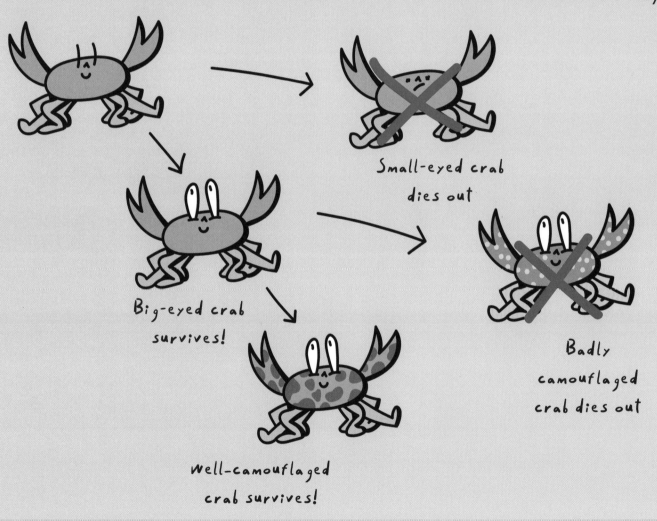

Small-eyed crab
dies out

Big-eyed crab
survives!

Badly
camouflaged
crab dies out

Well-camouflaged
crab survives!

Animals with not-so-useful features die out. This goes on and on for millions of years. It's like a competition where first prize is surviving and second prize is . . . er . . . not surviving. Awkward . . .

Eventually, very cool things can evolve. For example, the bombardier beetle has evolved two sacs full of toxic chemicals inside its guts. When threatened, it mixes the two chemicals together and farts a stinky, scalding-hot mixture at whatever's chasing it. Charles Darwin, one of the first people to write about evolution, took one of these boiling beetle bum-bombs to the face. Unlucky, Charles!

Chaz Darwin
(1809 – 1882)

Animal bodies (and bums) change to increase their chances of survival. But . . . OH NO! What if the environment they live in changes?

THE WORLD'S OLDEST FARTBOX

Okay, that's the entire theory of evolution covered . . . well, not really.
There's a lot more to say about how animals change over time,
but let's get back to bums!

We now know why bums are useful, but who actually had the first? One of
the oldest creatures that definitely had a bum was called *Ikaria wariootia*.
It was a tiny worm, about the size of a grain of rice, that squidged about in
the shallow parts of ancient oceans. A worm might not sound exciting, but it's
one of the oldest examples of an animal with a front and back end.

Finally, a bum!

Ikaria wariootia,
555 million years ago

Remember, we're talking about things that lived a REALLY long time ago. There might be older bums than this one, but we just haven't found them yet.

BUM HALL OF FAME

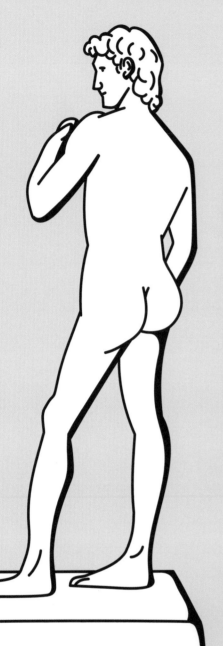

David
by Michelangelo

First bum
in space

Bumflowers
by Vincent van Chuff

Bun-titled

David!
Have you
no shame?

SO HOW DID BUMS TAKE OVER THE WORLD?

Up to this point, the planet looked very different from today's world. On land, there were no animals or plants, and life in the sea was much slower and simpler. The atmosphere didn't have much oxygen in it, and this stopped animals from getting big and complicated.

Until . . . **the Cambrian Explosion!**

Not that kind of explosion!

The Cambrian Explosion was when life really started to get going. We don't know exactly how or why, but more oxygen appeared, and from fossil records it looks like lots of new animals burst onto the scene. During this time, life went from slimy mats of bacteria and tiny worms to all sorts of exciting plants and creatures. And those exciting creatures had bums, too.

EXCITING!

THE BIG BANG OF BUMS

The creatures with bums did very well for themselves. As we've learned, having a bum means you can eat more and spend the energy on evolving new stuff. Now, because this helped animals survive, evolution started heading off down a much bummier route.

These early bum-owners were getting bigger— and tastier, too. It's around this time that we start to see real evidence of animal predators . . . like this terrifying giant shrimp thing, *Anomalocaris*!

530 MILLION YEARS AGO

Most animals today have a bum, so they can trace their family tree back to the Cambrian Explosion: **THE BIG BANG OF BUMS**.

BUMS TAKE OVER THE LAND

360 MILLION YEARS AGO

Most of what we've talked about so far has been underwater, where life began. But during this time, known as the Cambrian Period, plants started creeping up onto land. After a few million years, creatures that looked a bit like crabs and millipedes followed them up into the sunlight.

Then, 140 million years later, some fish started to drag their poopers up onto land, too. These fishy creatures were called tetrapods. They had four small legs and scaled skin, and they laid eggs. At first, their legs weren't very strong, but they soon got bigger.

Some of the best fossils of tetrapods were found in a place called Willie's Hole in Scotland. That's the only willy in this book, so enjoy it while it lasts!

1st time on the beach

REPTILIAN RUMPS

Over the next few million years, tetrapods evolved in lots of different directions. Some split off to become amphibians. Others evolved into reptiles like snakes, dinosaurs, and more. All of these creatures have a very special bum called a cloaca. A cloaca is an amazing, all-in-one, Swiss-Army-knife bum. You can do everything with it. You can poop out of it, pee out of it, mate through it, and even lay eggs out of it!

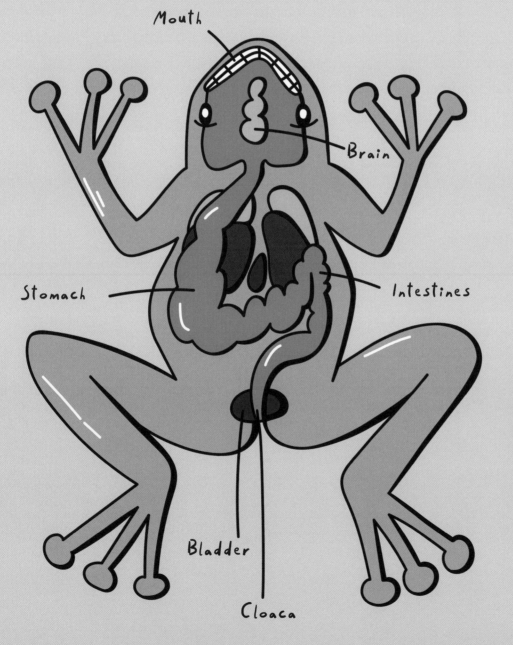

JURASSIC FART

Next, it was the age of
the cloaca-owning dinosaurs!

Dinosaurs had similar bums to crocodiles,
a living close relative. One of the
best preserved fossils of a dinosaur
drainpipe belonged to *Psittacosaurus*,
which had a leathery bum made of
two wrinkly, horizontal lips. Mwah!

120
MILLION
YEARS
AGO

THE HINEY THAT TIME FORGOT

Like modern crocodiles, some dinosaurs probably had smelly glands in their bums that sent messages to other dinosaurs. Messages like . . .

Hey! Let's make eggs together.

Get lost, weirdo.

???

But dinosaur bums are still around today . . . because not all dinosaurs died out. That's right! Some survived and became birds. Yep, birds are technically dinosaurs.

And, because they have cloacas, they poop, pee, and lay eggs all from the same hole. That's why bird poop is so wet . . .

. . . And also why you should always pick broken shells out of your fried eggs.

So next time you get pooped on by a seagull, you can pretend it was a tiny *T. rex*. And in a way, it was!

FURBALL EARTH

Next, a big ol' asteroid hit Earth.

It kicked a huge cloud of dust into the air, blocking sunlight and turning the planet cold. This was really bad for most of the dinosaurs and they died out, but it suited another type of animal well.

The mammals!

These creatures had four legs and a spine, just like dinosaurs. But they didn't have scales or feathers—they had fur instead. Perfect for chilly evenings in the Cenozoic period! As the dinos died out, the warm and snuggly mammals took over. And they had very different bums.

28

WHERE THE SUN DON'T SHINE

Dinosaurs and mammals both evolved from the tetrapods that we met earlier. But while dinosaurs laid eggs, most mammals evolved to grow babies inside their bodies. Dinosaurs were happy to do everything through their cloacas, but mammals evolved to poop from one hole and give birth to live babies out of a different one.

Both worked fine for millions of years, but when the asteroid hit, mammals had an advantage. A baby that grows inside a body can be kept warm, and is more likely to survive when it's cold outside. Mammals have kept their holes separate ever since!

But wait . . . One group of mammals lays eggs and squeezes poop out of the same hole. These very strange animals are called monotremes, and include platypuses and echidnas. They're the only mammals that have cloacas!

FOOD SO NICE THEY ATE IT TWICE (OR FOUR TIMES)

The period from the extinction of the dinosaurs to the present day is called the Cenozoic Era. During this time, mammals and birds took over Earth. Tough, stringy plants appeared, so mammals got bigger and evolved new stomachs to be able to munch on them. Grass-eating creatures often need lots of different stomachs to squeeze the last bits of goodness out of their food. Hippos have three stomachs, while cows, giraffes, and sheep all have four!

Other creatures, like rabbits, stuck to a single stomach, but have found a way to digest their food *twice*. How? Well, by eating their own poop, of course.

FIT FOR PORPOISE

We'll come back to bums in a hot minute, but for now—listen to this. The early Cenozoic coastline was a great place to catch tasty morsels. One land-based mammal called *Ambulocetus* got carried away and spent more and more time in the water. It got so much of its food from the water that it eventually turned its back on land entirely. It evolved into the sea-dwelling *Dorudon*, which, much later, evolved into the blue whale.

So . . . fish evolved into reptiles, which evolved into land-based mammals, which evolved into sea-based mammals, which, over time, evolved into the blue whale, the largest creature to have ever existed.

This is a great example of how weird evolution can be. Throughout all this time, creatures like jellyfish and squid barely changed!

MONKEYING AROUND

63 MILLION YEARS AGO

Back on land, another type of mammal appeared during the Cenozoic: the primates. They had a great time, and eventually branched off into lemurs, lorises, tarsiers, monkeys, and apes. Primates often live in groups, and like other creatures, some tell each other things with their posteriors. Because they have such complicated social lives, they have a lot to say and have evolved some colorful keisters to say it with!

Today, for example, mandrills live in big groups called hordes. When a male becomes the leader of his horde, his body changes. His face and bum swell up, and turn bright blue and red! This tells other males that he's in charge, and unless you want to pick nits off his back hair, you'd better clear off.

We'll come back to primates that live in groups in a little while, because one particular species is very special.

From here onward, Earth slowly started to look a lot more like it does now. Barring a few extinction events, life on Earth has been, well, vibing. And that pretty much brings us up to today!

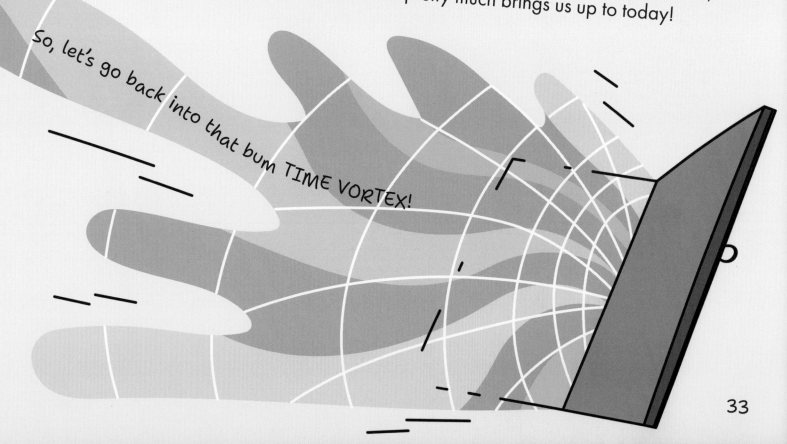

THE AGE OF THE ANUS

So, here we are, back in the present. A world ruled by bums!
Cat bums, gnat bums, bat bums, and badger bums. Blobfish
bums, seahorse bums, and blue-footed booby bums. Ninety-nine
percent of animals these days have a bum, and only a few bumless
creatures are holding out. Don't worry, we'll see them soon.

Cheeks

Rump

Fart
factory

Buns

Botty

Backside

Stink
spreader

36

NEW BUTTS ON THE BLOCK

Animals (and their bums) have completely conquered Earth.
They're all over the place, from fish in the deepest, darkest ocean
trenches, to migrating birds high up in the atmosphere. And sure,
everyone loves dinosaurs—but the animals that we have today
are up there with the greatest that have ever lived.

So, let's meet some of these modern marvels and their mudchutes!
In no particular order . . .

CRUSTACEAN CHEESE-CUTTERS

Crabs are in the same BIG group of animals as insects. We have hard shells called "exoskeletons." This means our "bones" are on the outside and our muscles are on the inside.

Having a shell means crabs poop in our own way. We're still a tube, but a curled one that starts at our mouth and ends in our chests. That's right—we poop out of our chests! Our hard shells mean we can't squeeze out poop like mammals can, so we have to reach into our bums and pull out poop with our claws.

Like this! HNNNNNGGHHHHH!

BUG BACKSIDES

Crabs' long-lost insect cousins get up to all kinds
of antics with their rear ends.

Many insects, like some
fungus gnats, have
glowing grunters, which
they use to attract prey
into sticky web traps.

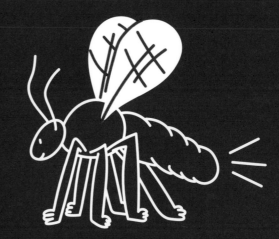

Glassy-winged sharpshooters use their
bums as catapults and fling droplets of
pee around at super-fast speeds!

Aphids make a sweet, sticky goo
inside their derrières, and ants like it
so much they farm them for it! The ants
look after the baby aphids, and in
return get all the bum-juice they can
drink. But who would want to drink or
eat anything that comes from a bum?

Well, lots of animals would—including humans! Just look at this next set
of muck spreaders if you don't believe us . . .

EAU DE TOILETTE

Who owns this furry farter?

It's a beaver! And hidden in a beaver's bum is a special gland that makes a sticky goo called castoreum. This goo (apparently) has a delicious earthy smell. Back in the olden days, it was used in perfumes and foods like vanilla ice cream. Don't worry, though—it's not used much any more.

WOMBAT COMBAT

Beneath its fur, a wombat's bum is made of thick plates of bone. It uses its mighty tush to dig a deep burrow and protect itself from predators. When it gets chased by a dingo, fox, or Tasmanian devil, a wombat will dive into its burrow and block the entrance with its bony behind.

That's the outside of a wombat's bum . . . but you want to know what's going on inside as well, right? Of course you do! Well, a wombat has very special muscly guts that squeeze its poop in different directions. When it goes to crimp one off, the poop comes out in cubes.

The wombat is the only animal we know of that has cube-shaped poops, but, like lots of things, we don't really know why. One idea is that it uses these homemade logs to mark its territory.

SEA CUCUMBERS IN A PICKLE

When sea cucumbers are attacked by crabs or fish, they squirt out a web of sticky goo from their poop chute. This confuses an attacker and usually gets them to leave. The goo is actually an organ and sea cucumbers have to regrow it every time. Yikes.

FART BOX
THIS WAY

But farting out goo doesn't gross everyone out. Like many animals, sea cucumbers breathe through their bums. Australian pearlfish hang around until the cucumber needs to take a breath, then they just slide right in. Up to fifteen pearlfish have been found living in one sea cucumber's bum! Aaargh!

BEACH BUMS!

Parrotfish eat coral, so that's what they poop, too. And over a really long time, their poop forms beautiful, white, sandy beaches that humans like to sunbathe and take selfies on. In fact, some beaches in Hawaii are about 70 percent parrotfish poop!

SQUID MARKS

Squid are soft, squishy animals called mollusks. They move by sucking water up into their bums and then blasting it out. Kind of like a jet engine! Their guts are connected to the jet, so when they scoot off, they make a kind of poop cloud. So, watch out for that if you ever chase a squid!

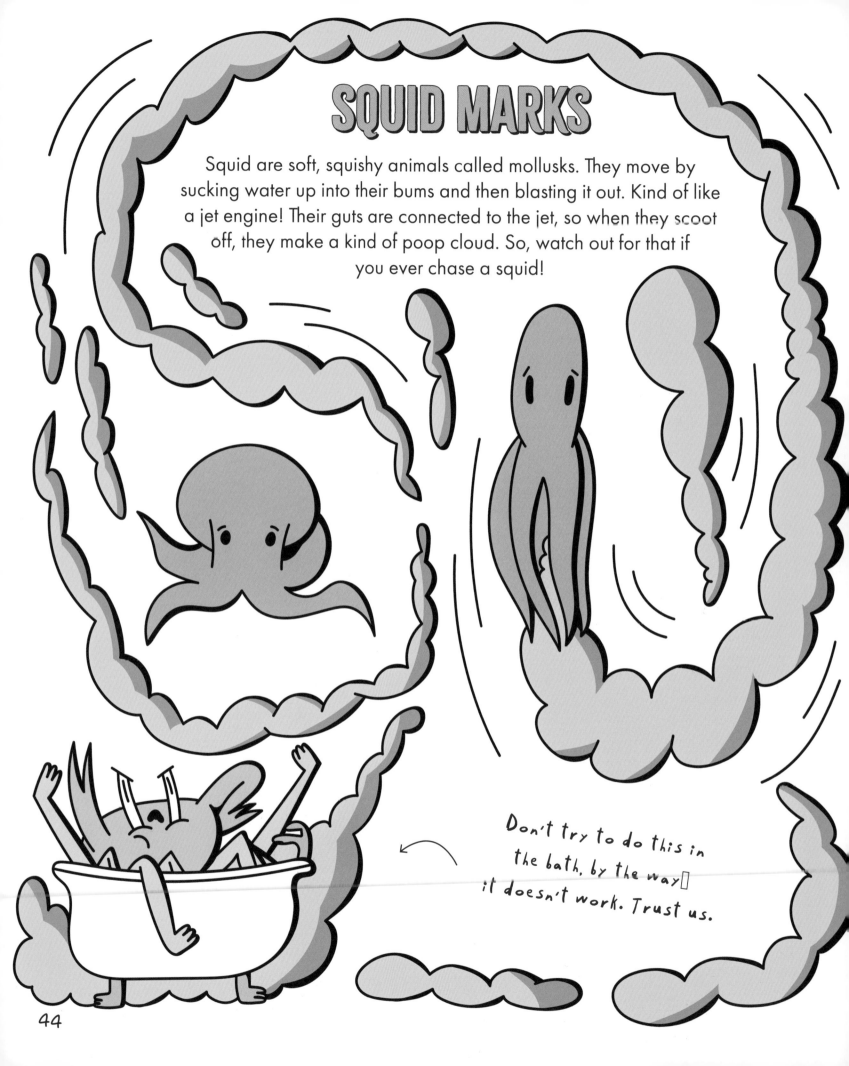

Don't try to do this in the bath, by the way — it doesn't work. Trust us.

SNAILY BUM-HEAD

Snails are also mollusks, but they don't use their bums to move around. Instead, a snail's caboose is above its head. Its guts curl around inside its shell, so food goes in the mouth, up, round, and back out of the top of the shell. It's a bit like you pooping out of the back of your neck!

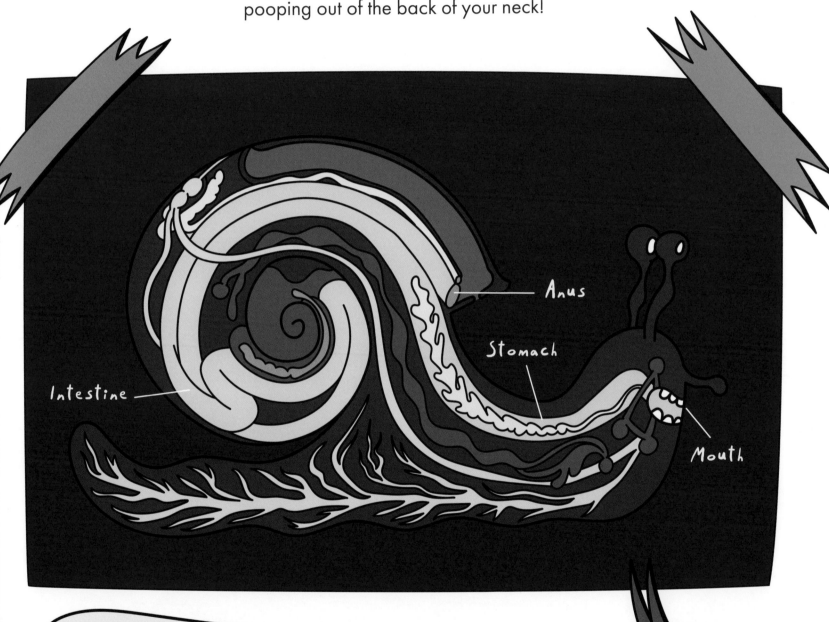

Intestine

Anus

Stomach

Mouth

Oh, and it breathes out of its anus, too. NICE.

RETURN OF THE FOOD BAG

Remember the food bags earlier in this book? Well, they never really went away! Some creatures are still stubbornly refusing to grow a bum.

The sea sponge—which is an animal, not a plant—eats by filtering water through thousands of tiny microscopic mouths. It just sits there at the bottom of the sea while food washes right through it, and its poop washes back out. Compared to a bum-owner, it doesn't eat much, but to stay alive, it doesn't need to! Sea sponges have been hanging around for a ridiculously long time. In fact, the first ever animal may have even been a kind of sea sponge. So, respect your elders!

BYE BYE, BOTTOMS

Creatures like starfish, sea urchins and sea cucumbers are called echinoderms. These weirdos are in all of the world's oceans, and have had bums since they showed up more than 520 million years ago. But some decided that bums just weren't working for them!

The basket star is an echinoderm that evolved back into a food bag. It catches tiny morsels of food with one of its many arms, stuffs them right into its stomach, and pukes or poops the waste back out of the same hole. Would it wipe with napkins or toilet paper?

TO BUM, OR NOT TO BUM?

If you thought the basket star couldn't make up its mind wait until you hear about the warty comb jelly! This ancient blob is an animal called a ctenophore, and while it looks a bit like a jellyfish, it's actually quite different.

For a long time, scientists had absolutely no idea where it pooped from. It was a real mystery until it was eventually caught on video.

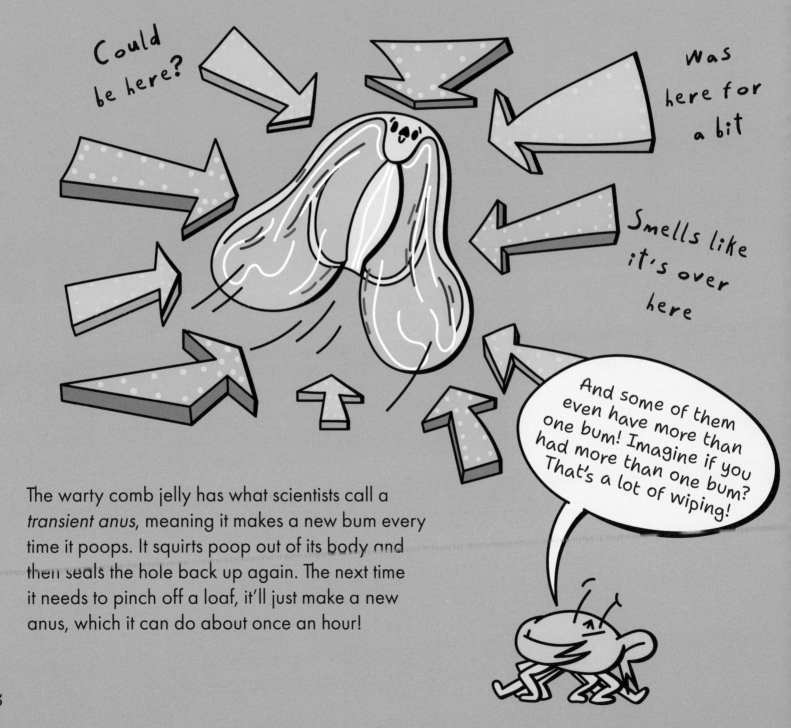

Could be here?

Was here for a bit

Smells like it's over here

And some of them even have more than one bum! Imagine if you had more than one bum? That's a lot of wiping!

The warty comb jelly has what scientists call a *transient anus*, meaning it makes a new bum every time it poops. It squirts poop out of its body and then seals the hole back up again. The next time it needs to pinch off a loaf, it'll just make a new anus, which it can do about once an hour!

BUTT WHY?

Maybe the warty comb jelly will settle down and get a "real" bum one day. But maybe it won't. Maybe it'll grow something else we can't imagine. We'll find out in a few million years!

What the basket star and the warty comb jelly tell us is that evolution is not a straight line. It's not about reaching some perfect body . . . because there's no such thing. Living beings change their bodies and behavior to survive. A bum might be useful sometimes, and other times it might just get in the way.

PLANET EARTH'S BIGGEST BUNS

It's time to talk about a very special bum . . .
the biggest on Earth.

So, who could be the owner of this magnificent corybungus?
Maybe an elephant? A giraffe? A bear? A hippopotamus?
What about a whale? The answer might surprise you . . .

YOU!

That's right! In proportion to its body size, humans have the biggest bums on Earth. Obviously, whale bums are bigger overall, but that's not surprising when you see how big whales are.

If a blue whale was shrunk down to the size of a human, the human would win in a big booty bum-off. Congratulations!

AND YOUR BUM

Human bums help you do something that's pretty unusual in the animal world: stand upright. Walking on two legs is tricky, and a lot of muscles are needed to hold the top half of your body up. And where are you going to put all those muscles? Your bum, that's where! Well, your bum cheeks, to be exact.

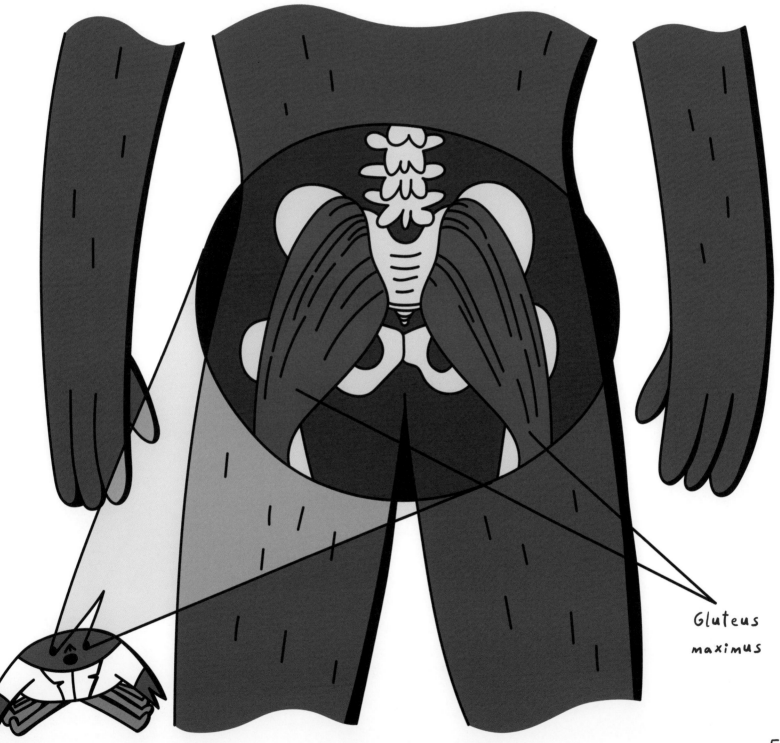

Gluteus maximus

WHY DO HUMANS HAVE SUCH BIG BUMS?

Humans evolved from apes. Over the last 7 million years or so, your ancestors gradually evolved to stand up, instead of living life hunched over like a chimpanzee (no offence, chimpanzees).

Standing upright rather than on all-fours freed up human hands for foraging, making tools, and taking care of babies. It made them look bigger so predators were less likely to try and eat them. It also let humans walk long distances and settle in new places. Big buttocks kept human bodies steady, and helped them move in ways that their primate cousins just couldn't.

APES VS HUMANS

The tailpipes of humanity's closest relatives, chimps and bonobos, are smaller and flatter because while they need powerful limbs for climbing trees, they don't need to stand upright.

Apes are always going to beat you to the top of that fruit tree. But you can walk much farther in a day, and your hands are free to carry snacks, write poems, or scratch your bum while you walk. If humans had never stood up, history would have been very different, and that's got a lot to do with your massive badonkadonk.

THE FUTURE OF BUMS

Evolution is always happening. So where will bums go next? Well, this recently discovered animal might know! Meet *Ramisyllis multicaudata*, a very strange worm. Its body branches off in different directions, with a bum at the end of each branch . . . so it can have up to 1,000 bums!

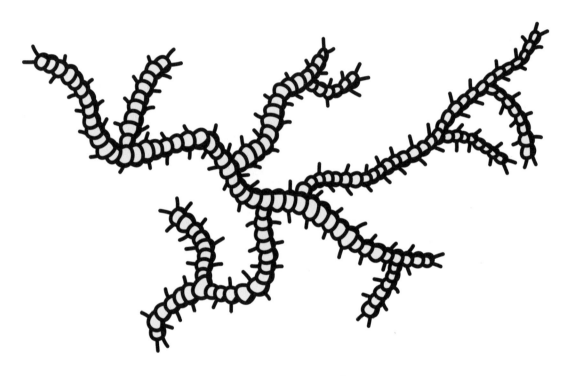

What do you think bums might look like in the distant future? Could humans end up with 1,000 bums, too? What would your toilets look like? There could be cyborg humans with robotic bums . . . or evolution could go in a totally different direction!

BUMS ACROSS THE GALAXY

And what about elsewhere in the universe? Would bums evolve the same way on an alien planet? Maybe. Maybe not! Perhaps aliens have evolved other ways of getting rid of their poop.

This, bum fans, is where science ends and your imagination takes over.

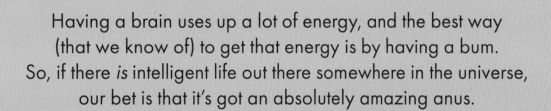

Having a brain uses up a lot of energy, and the best way (that we know of) to get that energy is by having a bum. So, if there *is* intelligent life out there somewhere in the universe, our bet is that it's got an absolutely amazing anus.

Maybe we'll find out one day!

LOVE YOUR BUM!

A world without bums might look like it did before the Cambrian Explosion; no animals on land and just squashy things floating around in the oceans.

Without bums, there would be no front ends or back ends. No eyes or noses or brains. There would be no birds singing, no laughter, and definitely no books about toot whistlers.

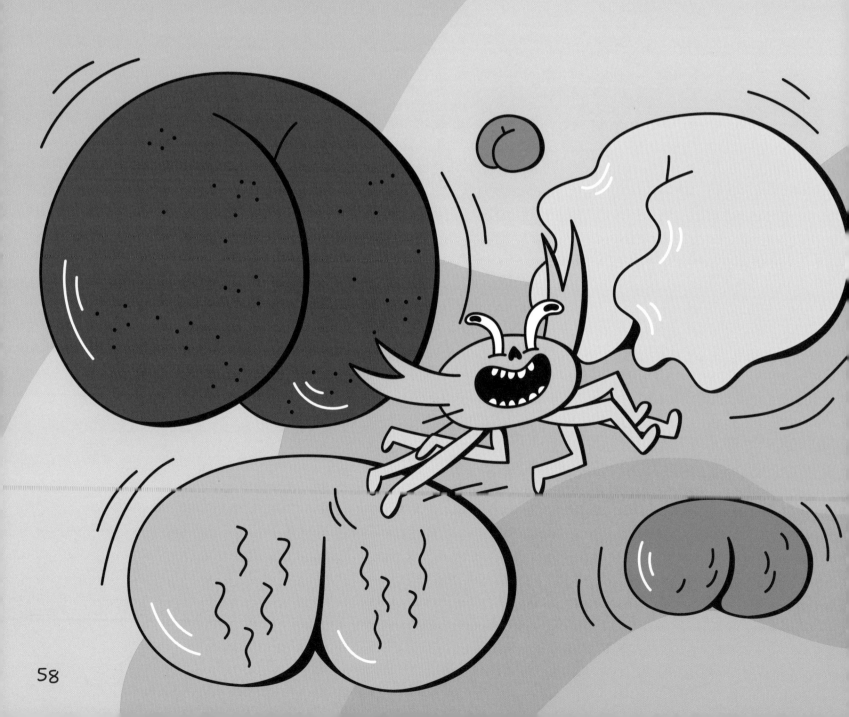

Yes, bums are pretty funny. But they're much more than that. They're one of the things that make humans *human*. They can explain how life has gone from blobs in the ocean, to the beautiful planet of stink trumpets that gave birth to YOU.

Your bum is useful. It's got a job to do and a story to tell. It lets you run and jump and dance and wave things around your head like the wild genius you are. There will never, ever be another one exactly like it. Whether it's big, small, pink, brown, wibbly, spotty, smooth, or hairy, your bum is an important part of the greatest story ever told: the evolution of life on Earth. If there were no bums, you wouldn't be here at all!

TIMELINE OF LIFE ON EARTH!*

*Not to scale

Four and a half billion years is a really long time, so there's a lot that we're not sure about. Maybe in the future, you could become a scientist and help fill in the blanks?

Big gap—not much happens. Booooring!

4.5 billion years ago
Earth is formed

4 billion years ago
Life begins

120 million years ago
When the Psittacosaurus lived

240 million years ago
Dinosaurs appear!

66 million years ago
Dinosaurs wiped out! Oh no!

66 million years ago
Mammals start taking over

50 million years ago
Ancestors of the blue whale go back in the sea

63 million years ago
Monkeys appear!